WE ARE PUSSY RIOT OR EVERYTHING IS P.R.

A PLAY ABOUT THE MOST FAMOUS PERFORMANCE ART PIECE IN HISTORY

BY

BARBARA HAMMOND

★

DRAMATISTS
PLAY SERVICE
INC.

WE ARE PUSSY RIOT OR EVERYTHING IS P.R.
Copyright © 2020, Barbara Hammond

All Rights Reserved

NOTE ON BILLING

SPECIAL NOTE ON SONGS/RECORDINGS

2

WE ARE PUSSY RIOT OR EVERYTHING IS P.R. was commissioned by the Contemporary American Theater Festival (Ed Herendeen, Founder & Producing Director; Peggy McKowen, Associate Producing Director), Shepherdstown, West Virginia, which produced the world premiere in 2015. It was directed by Tea Alagić, the set design was by Peter Ksander, the costume design was by Trevor Bowen, the lighting design was by D.M. Wood, the sound design was by Elisheba Ittoop, the video and projection design was by Matthew Haber, and the production stage manager was Deb Acquavella. The cast was as follows:

NADYA .... Libby Matthews
MASHA .... Liba Vaynberg
KATYA .... Katya Stepanov
FEMALE ROLES .... Sarah Nealis
FEMALE ENSEMBLE .... Allyson Malandra,
Keyla McClure, Brianne Taylor
SERGEI/PUTIN/MALE ENSEMBLE .... T. Ryder Smith
GUARD/MALE ENSEMBLE .... Cary Donaldson,
Adam Phillips

WE ARE PUSSY RIOT OR EVERYTHING IS P.R. was developed at Emerson Stage (Melia Bensussen, Producing Director; David Colfer, General Manager) at Emerson College, Boston, Massachusetts, opening on March 31, 2016. It was directed by Kenneth Prestininzi, the set design was by Corey Umlauf, the costume design was by Caroline Blatz, the lighting design was by Ali Witten, the sound design was by Anna Drummond, and the production stage manager was Alta Lewis Millard.

NADYA/PUSSY RIOT GROUP .... Ryanna Dunn
MASHA/PUSSY RIOT GROUP .... Allie Wittner
KATYA/PUSSY RIOT GROUP .... Isa Braun
SERGEI .... Riley Fox Hillyer
ANNA .... Monica Rosenblatt
PUTIN/PROSECUTOR/OTHERS .... Mitchell Buckley
PATRIARCH/HUSBAND/OTHERS .... Justin Masters

3

PUSSY RIOT GROUP/OTHERS .... Lily Richards, Clare Gomes,
Maria del Mar Fernandez Gonzalez,
Cat Yamishira, Jade Zaroff

WE ARE PUSSY RIOT OR EVERYTHING IS P.R. opened at Theatre Battery (Logan Ellis, Producing Artistic Director; Gianna Gargiulo, Associate Artistic Director; Rebecca White, Associate Artistic Director) in Kent, Washington, on August 5, 2017. It was directed by Logan Ellis, the set design was by Lex Marcos, the lighting design was by Amber Parker, the costume design was by Luna McMeen, the original music and music direction were by Matthew Reed, the dramaturg was Gianna Gargiulo, and the production stage manager was Cassie Neiss. The cast was as follows:

NADYA/ANON. P.R. .... Erin Bednarz
MASHA/ANON. P.R. .... Adera Gandy
KATYA/ANON. P.R. .... Sango Tajima
GUARD/PATRIARCH/
CEELO GREEN/TV HOST .... Charles Hawkins
REPORTER/ANNA POLITKOVSKAYA/
DOCTOR/ANON. P.R. .... Caitlin Macy-Beckwith
PROSECUTOR/SECURITY/RUSSIAN
LANGUAGE PROFESSOR/ANON. P.R. .... Kait Mahoney
DEVOUT WOMAN/
LIEUTENANT/ANON. P.R. .... Mandy Rose Nichols
DEFENSE/SECURITY/
MADONNA/ANON. P.R. .... Danielle Alexis Nicole Mitchell
SERGEI .... Joshua Hamilton
PUTIN/PYOTR/COSSACK .... Jesse Parce
ANON. P.R. .... Tiana Ross

SPECIAL THANKS

Thank you to Mike Lerner, the documentary filmmaker of *Pussy Riot: A Punk Prayer*, for his sage advice and introduction[s] to Pussy Riot. In Moscow, many thanks to the art collective VGLAZ, civil rights activist Anna Karetnikova, journalist Juliana Lizer, translator Maria Fomina, and especially to those colleagues whose safety depends on not being named here.

WE ARE PUSSY RIOT OR EVERYTHING IS P.R. received extensive workshop time and space at New Dramatists.

WE ARE PUSSY RIOT OR EVERYTHING IS P.R. received a workshop at Duke University, dramaturged by Jody McAuliffe.

FOREWORD

We Are Pussy Riot or Everything Is P.R. was prescient.

The play is rife with impudence, feminist discourse, and non-standard political resistance.

It's not pretty.

It's great theater for dressing up in neon stockings and funny ski masks and... Wait...

PAY ATTENTION.

Why this play is necessary, why it needed to be written is to be found in its heart, in its love for its martyrs.

LOOK THEM UP. DON'T FORGET.

The play's political heart was broken cycles ago, but it still insists attention must be paid.

Its heart birthed the cost of protest before our current flurry of girl-power plays.

PAY ATTENTION!

Say the name of the punk group.

WHAT PUNK GROUP!

Can't say it? It's too... too what?

It's not pussy that is radical or dangerous.

NOT PUSSY.

It's...

The RIOT in between the lines.

The riot in how Barbara Hammond turns research into an emotional reservoir.

You can be a theater artist and put on this play.

(Will you dare stage the play in its true state of rage and kindness.)

DON'T PLAY ALONG.

We Are Pussy Riot or Everything Is P.R. won't play along.

We Are Pussy Riot or Everything Is P.R. is a play.

What's a riot good for?

Absolutely nothing!

PAY ATTENTION.

PUNK.

Ken Prestininzi, director
February 2020

6

PLAYWRIGHT'S NOTE

In February 2012, less than six months after they formed, the Russian feminist art collective Pussy Riot uploaded their punk prayer "Virgin Mary, Chase Putin Away!" to the internet. The video was recorded, in part, on the altar of Moscow's Christ the Saviour Cathedral, where women are forbidden from standing, much less yelling, punching, and kicking the air. The world took notice—and so did the Kremlin and the Patriarch of the Russian Orthodox Church. Three of the group's anonymous members were hunted down, arrested, and put on trial for "hooliganism motivated by religious hatred."

As I write this essay, Vladimir Putin is rewriting the Russian Constitution so that he will remain in power for life. This does not come as a shock to anyone who has been paying attention to world politics. As Sergei says: "So he likes his job, who can blame him?"

We are in an era of strongmen who "like their jobs," and the question now facing society is: "What are we going to do about it?" This play shows what a small band of young women did in 2012, and I hope this play both keeps that action alive in our memories, and begins many late-night conversations on campuses, street corners, factories, offices, kitchens, and cafes about what each of us might do when faced with gross injustice and flagrant abuse of power.

Until 2014, Pussy Riot was a movement. After that, for better or for worse, it became a brand. Though fascinating in its own right, that brand is not what this play is about. It's about a narrow window of time where activist art, religion, and politics clashed on the world stage.

Pussy Riot said "fun can be a revolutionary act," but the truth is, their words and their actions were rigorous and disciplined. They were students of philosophy and history. They trained for these actions, rehearsed to be spontaneous, just as a play is rehearsed so as to seem natural and effortless.

Pussy Riot were inspired by the Holy Fools (yurodivy) of Russian history, and understanding the role of these yurodivy is key to understanding how to perform this play. Their purpose was to wake people up to what is going on around and within them. They are not partisan—they simply hold up a mirror to what we are becoming, or could become, if we are not vigilant. Sometimes that is better accomplished with a whisper than a scream.

Nadya has repeatedly said that it is impossible to compare Western feminism and its concerns to the concerns of Russian women. "Feminism that doesn't benefit men is not my feminism," she has said. Men are part of their movement. Pussy Riot may require its performers to be female, but they are fighting for the equality of all people, and Sergei is one of those forgotten people for whom they fight.

I realize that calling this "a play about the most important performance art piece in history" is, in itself, P.R., but there are times when art does change the world, or at least won't allow us to look away from the mirror it holds up to our society—in that way, all artists are called to be yurodivy. So when you rehearse this play, imagine that after opening night everyone involved will be taken to prison. In many places around the world, that is exactly what is happening. You are performing for them because they can't.

Barbara Hammond
January 2020

THE TROUPE

12 YURODIVY ("Holy Fools")

Here are two examples of different character tracks.

Example 1
(8 women, 3 men, 1 n/s)

Nadya

Masha

Katya

Defense/Madonna/Pussy Riot Member

Prosecutor/Russian Language Professor/Marilyn Monroe/
Pussy Riot Member

Judge/British Feminist Lecturer/Pussy Riot Member

Devout Woman/Lieutenant

Doctor/Anna P./Security 2/Pussy Riot Member

Sergei

Guard/Putin/Security 1

Patriarch/Pyotr/Cossack/Russian TV Host

Reporter/Pussy Riot Member

Example 2
(8 women, 4 men)

Nadya

Masha

Katya

Defense/British Feminist Lecturer

Prosecutor/Doctor

Judge/Anna P.

Devout Woman/Lieutenant/Russian Language Professor

Reporter/Madonna/Marilyn Monroe/Pussy Riot Member

Sergei

Guard/Security 2

Patriarch/Pyotr/Cossack/Russian TV Host

Putin/Security 1

The yurodivy playing Nadya, Masha, Katya, and Sergei should have no other roles for clarity's sake.

The director can experiment with assigning the doubling during auditions and/or rehearsals. The yurodivy should work together to make the play, and delaying the assignment of roles may be good for the collaborative process.

The Reporter is not one reporter, but the entire world press corps, and his/her/their accents should be from all over the planet. Also, having a single yurodivy play the Reporter helps weave the story together and takes the audience on the play's journey.

Lines to be assigned include those of the TROUPE (all yurodivy), the PUSSY RIOT MEMBERS (those cast as P.R.), the PRISONERS, and the CROWD. Lines with the stage direction *(Distributed.)* are to be divided up and given to one or more actors. Playing with different variations on how the chorus of voices are shared and assigned is encouraged.

In addition to these 12, there may be a conductor/foley operator/ choirmaster, who is also a yurodivy.

SETTING

The Motherland.

LOCATION

A confined open space.

A Cathedral, Police Station, Courtroom, Corridor of Power,
Prison Cell, City Streets, a Soviet-Era Kitchen, a TV Station,
Public Baths, a Concert, a Labor Camp.
The Public Square.
A Stage. The Internet.

NOTE ON TEXT

Much of the dialogue is inspired by trial transcripts and statements
by public officials, including Patriarch Kirill and Vladimir Putin,
all of which are broadly available on the internet.

Prison scenes are created from Nadya's, Masha's, and Katya's letters
from, and interviews about, the detention center and the penal
colonies where they resided before and after their sentencing.

Sergei was created based on political activists, prisoners, and artists
in Russia and particularly by the events that took place in Bolotnaya
Square on May 6, 2012, and the arrests that followed. All other
characters are fictions based on the thoughts and language from
interviews, studies, and articles of real academics, anarchists, soldiers,
policemen, and the Orthodox.

Madonna, of course, is Madonna.

Poetic license is rampant throughout the play.

We were searching for real sincerity and simplicity, and we found these qualities in the yurodstvo ("the holy foolishness") of punk.

—Nadya Tolokonnikova,
Pussy Riot founding member

WE ARE PUSSY RIOT OR EVERYTHING IS P.R.

IN THE LOBBY

Audience is barred from entering theatre.

The entire Troupe is in the lobby as audience members. Each has a piece of costume hidden that will identify them when the time comes.

There is a carnival atmosphere. It could go so far as having Pussy Riot supporters with climbing gear on the walls who hold up a sign that says: "TAKE MY PICTURE!"

Sergei hands out homemade flyers that read:

CONSTITUTION ARTICLE 31:
Citizens shall have the right to gather peacefully,
without weapons, and to hold meetings, rallies,
demonstrations, marches, and pickets.

He may wear a placard with this information as well.

Before people can enter theatre, a Pussy Riot Action breaks out.

A handful of brightly balaclavaed Pussy Riot members perform for a noisy, confused minute.

NADYA. *(Masked; shouting.)* Come, let us taste freedom together!
PUSSY RIOT MEMBERS. Church! State! Separate!
Choose the rhyme the priests will hate
Guns, tanks, arrows, bows
Mankind reaps the shit it sows!
Holy Shit!

> *One of the Troupe becomes the Cossack and whips the chanting*

Pussy Riot members. Other Troupe members pull on watch caps and become Security Forces, surrounding the audience and keeping a sweeping eye on them.

COSSACK. Get out of here. Get out of here while we ask you nicely!

PUSSY RIOT MEMBERS. Holy Shit! Holy Shit! Holy Shit!
Mother Russia release your daughters
Motherland protect your girls
Virgin Mary destroy Putin
Madonna become a Feminist!

Other members of Pussy Riot are in audience, filming everything.

COSSACK. I will teach you to love our country!

Cossack whips them.
They call out in pain.
Sergei gets close, films this with his phone.

No filming! No filming here!

Cossack whips them again.

SERGEI. They have the right to protest!

COSSACK. No one wants this chaos!

Sergei and Cossack tussle.

SERGEI. Don't hurt anyone!

Cossack whips Sergei, gets Sergei's hands behind his back.

COSSACK. Arrest this man!

SERGEI. What are the charges?

COSSACK. Assaulting an officer. Inciting a riot! Violating the social order.

PUSSY RIOT MEMBERS. *(Distributed, to audience.)* Please. Film him! It is allowed! Don't let him get away with it!

Riot, riot!!

Some of them run off or take off masks and blend back in with the crowd.
If cast is large enough, others are arrested too.
Maybe some audience members are arrested too.

COSSACK. All those here to cause trouble, troublemakers, disperse. Go home!

Cossack leaves with Sergei in custody.
Security 1 and 2 are left in charge.

SECURITY 1. If you are here for the show, ahem, for the trial, for the service—mmm, if you have a ticket, please enter here.

SECURITY 2. This way. This way, please, to ensure a seat.

SECURITY 1. Everyone follow the others!

SECURITY 2. Welcome in!

PUSSY RIOT MEMBERS. *(Distributed.)* They are taking all your names!

They know where you live!

SECURITY 2. Please. Citizens. Ladies and gentlemen!
Enter this way! Thank you.

PUSSY RIOT MEMBER. *(Imitating Security's tone and style.)* As never seen before! Right this way!

SECURITY 2. One at a time! There is room for everyone!

SECURITY 1. This is the way in. Please open your bags. Bags open.

PUSSY RIOT MEMBER. Show them all your stuff!

SECURITY 1. Bags, please. It is for your own safety.

PUSSY RIOT MEMBER. The trial of the century! Step right up!

> *Security ignores Pussy Riot's antics.*

SECURITY 1. It is time! Spasibo! Thank you. This way, please.

SECURITY 2. Everyone follow the others! Welcome in!

> *The audience is funneled into theatre. They are sent through makeshift metal detectors and to a table for bag inspection by the Troupe members playing Security Forces. Audience may be patted down, questions asked, empty your pockets, etc. Security Forces do not smile but are very polite. Security may repeat the following, like a TSA guard at an airport, repeating the message for each new group within earshot.*

SECURITY 1 and 2. *(Distributed, repeated.)* Turn off your mobile and noise-making devices.

No weapons.

No recording devices.

No whistling, shouting, or stamping of feet.

No clapping. No booing.

Take your feet off the seats. No smiling. No judging.

No whispering, no thinking. Please!

> *Audience is directed to seats. Women are asked to cover their heads and men asked to uncover theirs. Colorful scarves are provided to those women without head coverings. Explanation given to those who ask: courtesy, tradition, respect.*
>
> *At the same time, Pussy Riot members are secretly trying to get audience members to take a Pussy Riot balaclava instead of a traditional head scarf.*
>
> *Audience members should take their pick.*
>
> *The "Bogoroditse Devo" by Rachmaninoff ("A Prayer to the Virgin Mary") overwhelms the space.*
>
> *A jumble of masks, costumes, props are piled up in view of audience. Filled burlap sacks. Maybe a couple of wheelbarrows. A pile of scripts, even. As if everything had been hastily abandoned and could be reclaimed at any moment.*
>
> *Devout Woman, head covered, is on hands and knees, trying to collect the blood-soaked garments, uniforms, etc.*
>
> *When audience settles, music stops. Preferably, the music is created live, and all of the yurodivy take part. Otherwise, there should be a portable source of music that various Troupe members commandeer throughout the play in the struggle to decide where we are.*
>
> *The yurodivy introduce themselves to the audience. They start, understandably, with Pussy Riot.*

ANNA P. We, all of us,

> *She introduces the cast.*

are a troupe of yurodivy, or "Holy Fools."
We come from the Orthodox tradition of saints who strive "with imaginary insanity to reveal the insanity of the world."
NADYA. We,

She introduces Pussy Riot members.

are Pussy Riot. In February 2012 we uploaded our punk prayer "Virgin Mary, Chase Putin Away!" to the internet.

BRITISH FEMINIST LECTURER. This caught the attention of the patriarch of the Russian Orthodox Church.

The Patriarch is introduced.

PATRIARCH. Who brought it to the attention of President Vladimir Putin.

Putin coughs.

RUSSIAN LANGUAGE PROFESSOR. Three of this group's anonymous members—Katya, Masha, and Nadya—

Each are introduced.

LIEUTENANT. were hunted down, arrested, and put on trial.

MASHA. Unlike most pieces of theatre, which are conceived in the writer's imagination, what you are about to witness was stitched together from our trial transcripts,

PATRIARCH. and statements by public officials, like me, the patriarch

PUTIN. And me, the president

PYOTR. all of which are broadly available on the internet.

PUTIN. Even when I sing.

DEVOUT WOMAN. He's going to sing?

Madonna makes an entrance.

MADONNA. Even what Madonna says, Madonna actually said.

TROUPE. Madonna?!

SERGEI. I, Sergei Barbarov, am based on a professor who, along with many

TROUPE. Many

SERGEI. others, were put in jail for insisting on their right to protest.

NADYA. While the world watched our trial

MASHA. Others remained how we began:

KATYA. Anonymous. And with the passage of time

DEVOUT WOMAN. And time it will pass

KATYA. Pussy Riot is reduced to a symbol

NADYA. A mask

RUSSIAN LANGUAGE PROFESSOR. A pose

ANNA P. A foggy memory of a misunderstood moment

SERGEI. Lost in the crowd of disasters, natural and man-made, at the dawn of the twenty-first century.

MASHA. I wonder this:

DEVOUT WOMAN. I worry about this:

NADYA. If nothing changes, why try?

GUARD. If everyone is shouting, who will listen?

MASHA. And if everything is P.R. how will we know what to believe?

> *Katya, Nadya, and Masha exit.*

DEVOUT WOMAN. And what about our souls!

> *The Troupe scatters.*

Our souls!

> *Now the play can begin!*
> *The "Bogoroditse Devo" plays again.*
> *Reporter enters space and addresses the need to know what in the world is happening.*

REPORTER. We are not in a court. It seems to be a church. It seems to be a cell.

> *Now s/he really gets a look around.*

It seems to be a country.
The glint of sun through stained glass.
Also, hmm, there is blood everywhere.

> *The Devout Woman works harder.*
> *The audience has arrived too early!*
> *The church is not clean. No one should see this.*

> *A whispered plea from the Troupe!*

TROUPE. REMEMBER THIS IS TRUE
YOU MIGHT FEEL UNCOMFORTABLE
YOU MIGHT RUN FOR THE EXITS

PUSSY RIOT MEMBERS. *(Distributed.)* THERE WILL BE PROFANITY.

YOUR CHILDREN CAN TAKE IT.

THERE WILL BE BLASPHEMY.

GOD CAN TAKE IT.

SHOTS WILL BE FIRED.

DON'T LOOK AWAY.

WE BEG YOU NOT TO FORGET.

> *Sergei is alone in prison. He addresses the audience.*

SERGEI. Someone said all you need to be in a punk band is three chords and the truth.

Only it was argued that Pussy Riot did not know chords.

> *The Devout Woman confirms this truth.*
> *She is in her own world—the Church.*
> *Sometimes they hear one another, and sometimes they do not.*

DEVOUT WOMAN. I was there. Christ the Saviour Cathedral!

SERGEI. A stone's throw from the Kremlin.

DEVOUT WOMAN. Tchaikovsky played here. This very spot!

SERGEI. It was very short. You blink, and it is done.

DEVOUT WOMAN. But the damage was done!

> *Guard takes device from a Troupe member who won't stop taking pictures of the blood and crushes it under his foot.*

GUARD. No photos. No devices. Turn off your devices! Thank you.

> *The Guard now turns on Sergei.*

It was bad to curse and shout in a house of God.

SERGEI. Excuse me?

GUARD. This is not right for a church.

SERGEI. Forgive me, I— *(To Guard.)* You are listening!

> *Guard doesn't want Sergei to know he is listening to every word.*

GUARD. No.

SERGEI. Okay, you are only "protecting."

> *Guard pretends not to hear him.*

21

You know, if you go out and say "I love Putin" no one will arrest you. If it is not ironically said—

GUARD. I love Putin.

SERGEI. I know. It's okay.

GUARD. I'm warning you. I am Orthodox.

SERGEI. Okay.

GUARD. I know you are not.

SERGEI. How do you know?

> *The Patriarch enters, swinging his thurible.*
> *The smoke from the incense covers the blood.*
>
> *He is in his own world: the church.*
> *But it's not the church of the Devout Woman.*
> *They are on different planes.*
> *The Patriarch has the ear of the president!*

GUARD. The patriarch told us that Orthodox Christians don't attend protest rallies.

SERGEI. Ah. I see.

PATRIARCH. Russia is Russia because of the Orthodox faith, and the Orthodox are Orthodox because God gave us Russia. They cannot be unlinked.

> *The Troupe recounts some history for the audience.*

SERGEI. Once upon a time, long ago, in the year 862, Cyril and his brother, these Byzantine monks, bring the alphabet, they bring knowledge to all the Mongols, the Tartars... And then, oh God,

PATRIARCH. the chanting,

GUARD. the icons,

SERGEI. so much beauty,

> *The Devout Woman is cleaning.*

DEVOUT WOMAN. So much blood!

TROUPE. *(Distributed.)* In Stalinist times, tens of thousands of priests were shot.

(Shooting.) Pshhew! Psshew!

In Stalinist times, there were show trials.

A VOICE. Confess! Come clean!

Another Fool arrested.

TROUPE. *(Distributed.)* Citizens were given scripts to read from, with foregone conclusions.

Now everything is different.

Ha!

But there are scripts to follow.

Catechisms to memorize.

Words not to say.

Opinions not to post.

Views not to express.

Don't veer left.

Or right.

Do not think too much about it.

Go to the ballet! Go to the races!

Say nothing.

Cross your legs. Cross your fingers.

Open your legs! Stand your ground! Say what you think!

The Patriarch is still in church.

PATRIARCH. Remember. The first Revolutionary was Satan!

Patriarch exits.
Devout Woman cleans his exit footprints.

SERGEI. And remember, too, Russian revolutions do not end well.

TROUPE. *(All.)* Riot. Riot. Revolution.

(Distributed.) If we are polite, you won't watch.

If we don't entertain, you won't care.

But because we are provocateurs,

we will buy real estate in your minds.

Devout Woman wants the audience to know a thing or two.

DEVOUT WOMAN. Yurodivy were holy. They were fools for

23

Christic. *(To Pussy Riot.)* You are just fools. *(Then back to audience.)* Who gave them authority! Not the people!

GUARD. No one voted for them.

DEVOUT WOMAN. And this man—Why listen to him? He is a nobody.

SERGEI. Well, I am—was a teach—professor—of history. So, I have memorized the past—okay okay I have remembered much of what I have read from many sources.

> *He sees his predicament.*

I am no longer young. I know I know I look young but nevertheless.

DEVOUT WOMAN. You don't look so young, let me tell you.

SERGEI. In my lifetime, I have seen this new free markets, free speech, a new constitution—so many rights! Everything on paper looks good.

> *Prison Guard enters with his baton.*

But who knows for how long we have this? A new law can be written as we speak.

> *A new law is written.*

TROUPE. A new law!

> *The media keeps the curious public informed and explains everything.*
> *Thank heaven for journalists!*

REPORTER. The Duma moved to change the law on term limits, clearing the way for another six, even twelve, years for Vladimir Putin.

> *Pussy Riot doesn't like this.*
> *Putin does!*
> *Sergei takes a more sanguine approach.*

SERGEI. So, he likes his job, who can blame him?
The point is we still have freedom of assembly. And here we are: assembled! This is itself a victory!

> *And the Devout Woman has seen everything.*

DEVOUT WOMAN. President for Life! Why not? Nothing will change.

She gathers the last of the bloody garments, hiding them away.
Guard turns his baton, is he playing or testing?
Well, we have seen it used already.

(To Guard.) Let's have some music! We were in church! I want to pray.

He will not.

GUARD. Look around you. This is a prison.

DEVOUT WOMAN. I have been here all my life. Don't tell me what it is.

She looks around.
Sound from the lobby. From outside the theatre.

VOICE FROM CROWD. Freedom! Justice!

CROWD. Freedom! Justice! Freedom! Justice!
Freedom! Justice! Freedom! Justice!

The stage becomes the court where justice will be served, or at least mentioned from time to time.

Nadya, Masha, and Katya are here!

Nadya raises her shackled hands above her head in defiance, Masha and Katya follow suit.

Both Sergei and the Devout Woman—and the Guard—are overshadowed.

Sound from the lobby. From outside the theatre. Crowd sound could be enhanced on portable music device.

Freedom! Justice! Freedom! Justice!

VOICES FROM CROWD. *(Distributed.)* Masha, be strong!

Katya, good morning!

PYOTR. *(From crowd.)* Nadya, smile!!

CROWD. Freedom! Freedom! Freedom!

Clap, clap, clap.

Freedom! Freedom! Freedom!

Clap, clap, clap.

This repeats in a chant. Troupe members encourage the audience to join them in the chant.

25

The government officials go through the wardrobe offerings and find their costumes.

The Troupe have to rely on what they have available, which does not always meet their own hopes, dreams, and expectations, but, as in life, they make do.

The Patriarch and Putin bring out game of Russian draughts (checkers) and play quietly.

REPORTER. *(On camera.)* Three female punk rockers who derided President Vladimir Putin in a forty-eight-second protest in Christ the Saviour Cathedral are on trial today.
—and the whole world is watching.

Patriarch and Putin aren't, that's for sure.
They're playing draughts!

Their performance was part of the biggest opposition protests of Putin's twelve-year rule, ahead of his March election to a new six-year presidential term—
The case has also prompted a fresh discussion about links between the church and the Kremlin in predominantly Orthodox Christian Russia, where ties between church and state go back more than a millennium.

Sergei fills in the details.

SERGEI. Ties that go back to the year 988—when Vladimir the First made all the citizens of Kiev gather on the banks of the river to be baptized—or face the consequences!

DEVOUT WOMAN. Vladimir—our first saint!

SERGEI. Nevermind he did make many wars kill many many… his brothers, even his sons—

TROUPE. How many?

SERGEI. Maybe no one counts, no one knows…

The Defense Lawyer grabs his brief. The Prosecutor, his satchel. The Judge, in her robe and holding a cudgel, presides between them.

It is all a play.
Commotion—stomps and whistles.

26

CROWD. Shame! Shame! Shame! Shame!

Again, Troupe can engage audience in this chant.

JUDGE. I am warning you all! This is not a theatre!

Crowd responds!
Drumroll.

Nadezhda Tolokonnikova, contemporary artist, wife, mother, shoplifter, "philosopher," and criminal ringleader:

Cymbal crash!

Guilty!

Nadya does not avoid her moment.
Drumroll.

Maria Alyokhina—insignificant young student—mother—wife—daughter, canvasser, sign-holder, petition-signer, tree-hugger, vodka drinker!

Crash of cymbal.

Guilty!

Masha does not look surprised.
Drumroll.

Guilty! Katya Samutsevich! Punk activist. Protester. Feminist. Admits she does not long for motherhood or marriage. Even her father thinks she is a—

Cymbal crash!

KATYA. NOT Guilty!

JUDGE. *(With certainty.)* Guilty.

The Judge and Prosecutor pack up to go.

DEFENSE. But no one has read out the charges.

JUDGE. Oh.

DEFENSE. We have not begun.

JUDGE. Oh.

Judge considers this.
Sergei tells it like it is.

SERGEI. So, we exaggerate. Forgive us! They had a trial. Very tedious. August. Hot. Everyone perspiring. It is all on the internet—you can watch it at home on your couch if you are curious—with a bowl of chocolates on your lap!

My trial, I guarantee, probably your trial, will not be filmed.

Perhaps we are not so photogenic.

> *The Reporter does a quick stealth interview before the real trial!*

REPORTER. You are behind bars, but you are laughing, smiling. What do you say to those who say you are mocking the court as you mocked the Orthodox?

NADYA. Play—fun—can be a revolutionary act.

REPORTER. What do you say to the Westerners who insist on thinking Pussy Riot is a punk band?

KATYA. We do not tour, we do not sell records. We are against all these things.

REPORTER. What—exactly—is Pussy Riot?

MASHA. We have been called everything. I don't care. I could call them a few things too.

REPORTER. So you are Defiant.

KATYA. Pussy Riot is an idea. You can't put an idea in jail.

NADYA. Many people on the outside support us. We are making contact with like-minded people everywhere.

REPORTER. Like-minded?

NADYA. Thinking people who care about human rights: for women, for LGBT, and for everyone who is not conforming to the mold.

REPORTER. Yet you are reviled here at home.

PUSSY RIOT MEMBERS. That's not true!

MASHA. So what?

We will outlive them.

We are young, they aren't.

REPORTER. What do you say to people who say your music is—terrible?

NADYA. We don't want to be good.

We want to be heard.

> *Return to trial as Pussy Riot comments on the charges.*
> *Everything is paced at a crawl of bureaucratic expediency but*

Nadya is taking it global.

NADYA. Look at us, we are in a cage. I hear the press and even the court calls this—glass jar—where we are on display twelve hours a day—an "Aquarium"! Who thought this up? You think we are fish?

KATYA. We are not.

NADYA. How are we supposed to breathe in here?

KATYA. Or think?

MASHA. *(With irony.)* Or pray?

She takes over for Nadya.

And over there we have our prosecutor, our lawyer, and our judge. We have not lied once, and the prosecution has lied over and over again.

KATYA. They can only say what the censors allow them to say. Maybe they don't even think we should go to jail—

NADYA. but they aren't allowed to say it—

PROSECUTOR. Who told them they could speak?—

DEFENSE. I want to read into the record the defendants' comments on the charges.—

MASHA. I ask for a continuance on the grounds that we have asked repeatedly but have not been allowed to meet with our attorneys.—

JUDGE. *(Indicates Defense.)* This IS your attorney!

Masha is unmoved.

MASHA. Yet we have not been allowed to meet and also we have not been given time to read the court transcripts—

Sergei offers an aside.
The court doesn't hear or recognize him.

SERGEI. Have any of us been allowed to speak to our attorneys?

TROUPE. No!

SERGEI. To see the transcripts on which to mount our defense?

TROUPE. No!

The Judge does not acknowledge the world outside the court.

JUDGE. *(To Masha.)* No more interruptions!

The Judge is serious.

There will be no continuance. Proceed.

MASHA. We have not—

DEFENSE. I want to read into the record the defendants' comments on the charges.

JUDGE. We have not yet heard the charges—

DEFENSE. Yet they wish to respond.

> *A beat.*

JUDGE. To what?

DEFENSE. Do you have any basis for denying my motion?

> *Judge sputters.*

JUDGE. This is—

> *The Defense will not have this chance again and leaps at it.*

DEFENSE. In that case we shall read them into the record.

DEFENSE and NADYA. We believe that art should be accessible to the public—

> *Nadya takes over, but Defense continues to try to read her statement for her. Nadya wins.*

We have performed in many venues—

NADYA. in Moscow—
on the roof of a bus,
in the metro
in front of Special Detention Center Number One—
in clothing stores—
and we were received with humor everywhere.

KATYA. We aren't criminals.

MASHA. We are political prisoners.

NADYA. They keep telling us that if we admit guilt, we will be released. But Pussy Riot does not lie.

> *An argument breaks out amongst Troupe. All hear one another even if they don't agree.*

DEVOUT WOMAN. Come, girls, you desecrated a holy place, you insulted Russia, say you're sorry!

KATYA. We have apologized!

GUARD. No one believes you.

DEVOUT WOMAN. Say it with remorse! You'll be home in time for tea! Mend your ways!

DEFENSE. *(To Judge.)* Our clients won't admit guilt. A call for that is pointless.

PUSSY RIOT MEMBER. The cathedral isn't holy. God isn't there.

DEVOUT WOMAN. Bite your tongue!

PUSSY RIOT MEMBERS. *(Distributed.)* It is a symbol of power and patriarchy!

Putin and the patriarch!

That's why we chose it.

SERGEI. In 1931, Stalin decided this cathedral had to go and—boom!—like that they blow it up and then built a swimming pool—

> *All swim.*

GUARD. My grandmother met my grandfather there. It was the biggest swimming pool in the world.

DEVOUT WOMAN. I learned to swim there. It was a sight to behold!

SERGEI. When the Soviet Union broke apart, when these girls were children, it is decided we need prayer more than exercise! And stopped the swimmers in their tracks as, brick by brick, they began again—

> *All build.*

PATRIARCH. There is no future if we desecrate our holy places.—

SERGEI. Imagine the millions and millions of rubles to rebuild such an edifice?

PATRIARCH. *(Addressing Guard and Devout Woman.)* No Orthodox can say this does not concern me—

NADYA. *(Aside to Defense.)* Are they going to give us five years?

DEFENSE. *(To girls.)* I doubt it will be five years.

NADYA. *(To Defense.)* Three years then?

DEFENSE. *(To girls.)* It is a possibility. We've already heard you will be killed in Siberia.

> *Back to court and the riveting trial.*

PROSECUTOR. *(To court.)* They made statements before I even read out the charges!

DEFENSE. The judge allowed it.

PROSECUTOR. It was my turn to speak!

DEFENSE. Well—

PROSECUTOR. They are attention seekers! Every word is now on the internet!

The Defense is tapping away, putting everything on Facebook.

JUDGE. Then read out the charges! Hurry!

Prosecutor is stuck on the disorder of the proceedings.

PROSECUTOR. *(To Defense.)* You realize there is now no defense— your clients just admitted that they are part of this group and that they performed in the cathedral?

JUDGE. Prosecutor, move on!

MASHA. I ask that the case be returned to investigators because of numerous inaccuracies and omissions in the documents.

The Devout Woman cannot stay silent.

DEVOUT WOMAN. *(Aside.)* Who does she think she is?

TROUPE. Shh!

DEVOUT WOMAN. If I have something to say, I will say it!

Back in court.

JUDGE. Motion denied. Prosecutor, read out the charges.

PROSECUTOR. *(Rapid-fire, at times unintelligible.)* Sometime before February 17, 2012, the three young women before you now, and other persons unknown to us, entered into a conspiracy for the purpose of rudely disrupting the social order in a manner that would express a clear lack of regard for societal norms, motivated by hatred and enmity, motivated by hatred for a particular social group, in the form of carrying out offensive actions inside a religious institution aimed at attracting the attention of a broad spectrum of citizen believers.

During this, the cathedral performance is reenacted.

They distributed roles among themselves and purposefully acquired clothing to be worn, clothes that clearly contradicted church norms, discipline, rules, and regulations inside the church. They then used balaclavas to disguise their identity, thus making it more difficult for them to be charged. This increases the gravity of their deed and makes it look like a well-planned act of malicious intent, meant to denigrate the feelings and beliefs of the numerous disciples of the Orthodox faith and diminish the spiritual foundation of the state.

DEFENSE. The charges are absurd! It's as if they jaywalked and are being charged with ruthless hatred for traffic! As if they were drunk and disorderly and were charged with deep-seated fury towards vodka!

JUDGE. Stick to the topic at hand.

DEFENSE. Don't tell me what to do!

NADYA. Think about what hatred is! We promise we do not have it!

DEFENSE. My clients require something to eat, water, the ladies' room. They are woken at five, brought here without breakfast, and kept in that stifling cage.
According to international law, this constitutes torture!

JUDGE. Stick to the topic at hand!

DEFENSE. What are the words "repent" and "God" and "sin" doing in this court?
Have you all forgotten we have a secular constitution and live in a secular government?

MASHA. *(Lashing out.)* I want to have a confidential meeting with my attorney! I have asked and asked—I want to draw attention to this!

JUDGE. You'll have your say. Right now I'm asking you if you understand the charges.

MASHA. I don't.

JUDGE. The prosecutor just read out the charges. What you are being charged with.

MASHA. I don't understand.

> *Sergei addresses court, who still do not notice him.*
> *He is in the wrong room. He is in prison.*

SERGEI. Also, the charges against me are baseless and I do not understand.

JUDGE. *(To Masha.)* What don't you understand? Please clarify.

MASHA. I just did.

JUDGE. Do it again.

Sergei acts as if it was he that was asked.

SERGEI. Like these girls, the entire incident was on tape. It is hard, in this internet time, for police to make up a story. But still they are tempted to do so, and they do it! The phenomenon is worldwide.

Masha addresses court.

MASHA. The prosecutor claims to be a mind reader. How does he know why we did what we did? He is ignoring our reasons and making of his own.

JUDGE. Fine. Sit down.

Prosecutor. Explain.

PROSECUTOR. Your Honor, the charges were read out. The charges are clear.

JUDGE. Now do you understand?

MASHA. No, he read out a small excerpt out of 140 pages.

JUDGE. It was a summary!

MASHA. I insist the entire indictment be read out.

No one wants to hear all that. A collective moan.

JUDGE. The prosecutor has outlined the charges.

MASHA. But I don't understand what the charges are based on.

JUDGE. He'll explain all that later.

MASHA. That doesn't help me understand. I have nothing to add.

Defense laughs.
Katya stands up.

KATYA. The charges don't make sense.

JUDGE. All right, so that's what you think.

The Guard speaks to Sergei in the quiet of prison cell.

GUARD. You beat a policeman.

SERGEI. Is that what you heard?

GUARD. We'll make sure you get what you asked for.

SERGEI. I did not beat a policeman.

GUARD. There is video.

34

SERGEI. Have you seen it?

GUARD. I don't need to see it.

SERGEI. If you watch you will see I did not beat anyone.

GUARD. If you get convicted, you really have it coming to you. The guards in the labor camp are no joke.

SERGEI. Who knows. I have never been there. Have you?

GUARD. No.

SERGEI. So we don't know.

GUARD. You should be on your knees. Praying for help.

SERGEI. Many thanks to you but religion it is always a little bit dangerous—sometimes you suffer. Sometimes you torture. I am better without.

> *Guard gives plate of food to Sergei.*

GUARD. Eat.

SERGEI. No.

GUARD. Eat.

SERGEI. I want to see a doctor.

> *Out of Sergei's sight, the head of the prison isn't happy. The Lieutenant and Sergei speak but don't hear one another. The Guard is stuck in the middle, hearing all. It is as if the Lieutenant's voice is stuck in Guard's head.*

LIEUTENANT. No one likes a martyr.

SERGEI. And I make yet another demand to see the transcripts of the case against me, so I can prepare for my trial.

LIEUTENANT. Tell him the martyrs are all dead.

SERGEI. I am a teacher. I was handing out educational pamphlets.

GUARD. It was an anti-government rally.

SERGEI. Yes. You can't force me to eat.

GUARD. We'll see.

SERGEI. International law states clearly that—

GUARD. No one is paying attention.

SERGEI. I have one demand—

LIEUTENANT. Beating a police officer. Inciting mass riots.

SERGEI. I want to see my attorney and I want the time to review my case with him.

LIEUTENANT. So you feel wronged? So you stop eating?

GUARD. That is a sin against your own stomach!

SERGEI. Countless times religion has sinned against people's stomachs! Time and time again!

Back in the drab, tense court.

JUDGE. Tolokonnikova? Do you plead guilty?

She is not yet with the court... maybe she is working on some statement she wants to make.

NADYA. *(Almost to herself, but also a plea.)* There is too much hatred in this country.

JUDGE. Tolokonnikova?

Nadya is back.

NADYA. No, I do not plead guilty. Can I explain?

JUDGE. You'll explain later.

NADYA. But I want everyone to understand.

JUDGE. You have pled not guilty. We are trying to establish your identity! State your full name.

Nadya does not answer.

I said state your full name. Your name!

Back in Sergei's world, the prison doctor arrives to examine Sergei. Guard checks her papers.

DOCTOR. Good morning. Name?

SERGEI. Yes.

DOCTOR. What is your name?

SERGEI. No one has asked my name for so—

DOCTOR. What is it?

SERGEI. Sergei.

A beat.

What is yours?

Doctor ignores him.

Nurse Olga? Nurse Bella?

DOCTOR. Doctor.

SERGEI. Ah. Finally I merit a doctor. I am moving up.

> *She checks his vitals.*
> *Writes everything down.*

"Do no harm," is that right? The international dictum of your profession.

DOCTOR. Tell me where you are.

> *She performs routine examination.*

SERGEI. Ah, hello. Oh, tickles.

DOCTOR. Do you know where you are?

SERGEI. More or less.

DOCTOR. Date of birth?

SERGEI. 10 September 1961.

DOCTOR. What is your occupation?

SERGEI. I was—I am a teacher.

DOCTOR. How do you feel?

SERGEI. So-so.

> *Doctor goes through warning signs for a hunger striker.*

DOCTOR. Are you faint?

> *Sergei responds.*

Headaches?

> *Sergei responds.*

Mood swings?

> *Sergei responds.*

Hungry?

> *Sergei responds.*

Step on scale.

SERGEI. Hmm.

> *Sergei steps on scale.*
> *Doctor writes down result.*

DOCTOR. How many kilos did you weigh when you arrived?

SERGEI. I don't remember exactly. I don't keep track.

DOCTOR. How long have you gone without food? How many days?

> *Masked Pussy Riot member pulls focus back to Pussy Riot.*
> *After all, the play is about them.*

PUSSY RIOT MEMBER. After our action in the cathedral, we went into hiding. We destroyed our cell phones, hid all the evidence, our dresses, our balaclavas. We didn't know what the others were doing—They arrested them one by one—

NADYA. Nadya,

MASHA. Masha,

KATYA. then Katya—

MASHA and KATYA. They even tried to arrest Nadya's husband, Pyotr,

PYOTR. but they let me go.

PUSSY RIOT MEMBER. They never got me.

> *Nadya, Masha, and Katya reenact their arrest.*
> *Masha, Katya, and Nadya are in separate interrogation rooms in police station.*
> *The Lieutenant is talking to all of them.*

LIEUTENANT. What is your name?

KATYA. Irina Loktina.

NADYA. Simone de Beauvoir.

MASHA. Selina Kyle.

LIEUTENANT. I said: What is your name, the name your parents gave you when you were born?

> *Outside police station, Pyotr, Nadya's husband, is pacing—he has three smartphones going at once.*

PYOTR. They're in the station getting roughed up right now! Oh God! Who should we contact first?…
Call a lawyer—sure, we should get them a lawyer—but what about the press? …Yes, listen to me—they arrested them!… No shit. I'm taking a picture of the police station right now. I'll tweet it.

> *Inside police station.*

MASHA. Aphra Behn.

NADYA. Simone de Beauvoir.

KATYA. Selina Kyle.

LIEUTENANT. Are you sure? I am asking you again.

KATYA. Yes, I am sure.

LIEUTENANT. You don't want to tell me your real name?

KATYA. It is my real name.

LIEUTENANT. All right, we will make a lineup.

> *Defense pulls Kat aside.*

DEFENSE. Tell me your name.

KATYA. Who are you?

DEFENSE. Your defense attorney.

KATYA. Where did you come from? Who hired you?

DEFENSE. You will be in big trouble if you keep lying to the cops.

> *The girls don't respond.*

What do you think, you can say whatever you want because you are girls? They will throw the book at you.

KATYA. We could not have stayed silent.

> *A beat.*

It was an unacceptable situation.

DEFENSE. What, exactly, was unacceptable?

KATYA. Putin expects transcendental guarantees for a long tenure at the pinnacle of power.

DEFENSE. Excuse me?

MASHA. The patriarch wears a forty thousand dollar watch while most families live on the edge of poverty.

NADYA. Someone has to call out the thieves and sexists.

DEFENSE. Oh.

> *He is just trying to do his job.*

LIEUTENANT. Line up!

> *Guard assists Lieutenant. Five girls line up.*
> *They adjust their clothing.*

They stare out.
The rest are invited to examine them, looking for recognizable features.

DEFENSE. This is pointless—they were wearing masks.

LIEUTENANT. They will be identified.

DEFENSE. By their knees?

LIEUTENANT. By their calves, if necessary. *(To girls.)* Turn around—ladies, please! Now.

Girls turn.
The Troupe whisper and point to the girls' calves, identifying Nadya, Katya, and Masha.
Guard moves to arrest them; Lieutenant stops him.

LIEUTENANT. Now. Dance.

NADYA. What?

DEFENSE. What?

LIEUTENANT. Kick, scream, punch. You know how to do it.

They stand still.

DEFENSE. This is ludi/crous—

LIEUTENANT. You know one another, yes?

They all look at one another.

It is clear that you know one another! It does you no favors not to talk.

They stand still.

Happy to scandalize the priests, the old-timers! Not so brave with those who will fight back. I see.

Nadya starts to speak, Masha squeezes her hand. Nadya pulls her hand away.
Nadya, Katya, and Masha are pulled from lineup and put in handcuffs.

That's that, then. Now tell me your real names! I am losing patience.

DEFENSE. It won't help you to lie now.

NADYA. We don't lie.

LIEUTENANT. Tell me your name.

NADYA. Nadezhda Tolokonnikova.

KATYA. Yekaterina Samutsevich.

Lieutenant looks at Masha.

LIEUTENANT. You don't have a name?

MASHA. Tell me the reason—

LIEUTENANT. I know your mother's name. Even your son's name. Why won't you tell me yours?

MASHA. My son—you know my son's— *(Mumbles.)* Maria Alyokhina.

LIEUTENANT. Speak up!

MASHA. Maria Alyokhina.

Lieutenant sits back. Mission accomplished.

LIEUTENANT. Maria, you are under arrest. Next time it won't be so easy for you. I promise.

Girls are led offstage by security forces, each in a different direction.

The problem is no one understood your protests. Next time go protest where you'll be understood!

MASHA. *(Whisper-shouts.)* Please stick together, you guys! See you soon.

NADYA. *(Whisper-shouts.)* Punk's not dead!

She tries to raise a fist, but the handcuffs stop her. The girls muffle their laughter as they are led away back to court.

Pyotr, Nadya's husband, is lingering outside police station. The foreign Reporter has already arrived with a film crew.

PYOTR. There they are—Nadya! Film that—see?
Look at them… Wow. Nadya—smile.

He is filming it himself too with his phone.

Film everything. It's okay. I'm her husband.

And the trial continues. Court is in session.

JUDGE. Attention! Come to attention everyone! I will now read aloud the conclusions of a committee of psychiatrists and psychologists who examined the defendants. Each was found sane and fit for trial but each was concluded to have a personality disorder.

Maria Alyokhina suffers from emotional distress brought on by her desire to protest. Nadya and Katya both are suffering from "mixed personality disorder." Nadya's symptoms are her "active position" in life and "heightened ambitions," and Katya—you exhibit an abnormal "insistence on your own point of view."

Nadya, Masha, and Katya can't believe it.

Alyokhina, do you plead guilty to the charges?

MASHA. I can't plead. I do not understand the charges.

A beat.

JUDGE. You are college-educated! You are literate.

MASHA. I have not yet finished college. And I am not a lawyer. I can't—

JUDGE. Answer the question!

MASHA. *(Quickly, efficiently—for the record.)* I plead not guilty to the crimes described in Article 213, Part 2. I also believe that in reviewing a case filed under this article, ideological aspects are as important as facts, because the arguments rest on motivation and the motives of our actions stem from our ideologies. The prosecution is trying to play down the political and creative components, which are in fact key here.

Devout Woman is transfixed by trial, though no one notices her.

DEVOUT WOMAN. Now she thinks she's a lawyer!

Masha, the girl who said she did not understand, understood.

MASHA. Despite your accusations, we aren't saying this for attention—we are saying it for all of you—

Masha sees the Devout Woman.

so you will hear us. I realize this is difficult when politics infects us all with suspicion and hatred, but we must try, very hard, to listen to one another.

Applause from Nadya and Katya and others.

Back in the privacy of the prison, Sergei still has not had his day in court.

GUARD. You mind your own business, you will not suffer.

SERGEI. Excuse me?

GUARD. You go to work, and come home for dinner, and don't stand on street corners in the freezing cold handing out pamphlets.

SERGEI. But it is permitted.

GUARD. You were in the wrong place at the wrong time.

SERGEI. Who in this world is so lucky as to be in the right place at the right time?

> *He looks around him.*

Well. I suppose there are many.

GUARD. My father fought in Afghanistan and lost an eye. My grandfather died in the Great Patriotic War.

> *A moment of respect.*

SERGEI. *(More quietly.)* But it is permitted.

GUARD. But you are here, locked up.

SERGEI. I suppose they don't like what the pamphlets say.

GUARD. Then why write such a pamphlet.

SERGEI. It's Article 31 of the Constitution. I didn't write it.
I don't know if you will understand.
You never disobeyed your parents, your teachers?

GUARD. When I did, I was punished.
If I was caught.

> *Devout Woman can hear what is happening in the prison too. And wants to be heard.*

DEVOUT WOMAN. And it's a good thing! Who wants all the young people to be hooligans?

> *The Devout Woman's entry into the prison space gives the whole Troupe access to Sergei and his words, if only for a short while.*

SERGEI. If we are civilized people, enlightened people, you know who we have to thank for that?
Peter the Great! Yes, he traveled a great deal and when he came home he declared Russia is very backwards—so first he ordered to everyone just to change clothes to European clothes.
And if you are a peasant yes, you can have beard, but if you are a merchant you must pay taxes for your beard and if you are a noble

43

you just will be killed if you have beard—yes, yes!

Also, he decided "Let's change year!" and overnight it was 1700—like in Paris. What a guy!

GUARD. You really like history.

SERGEI. Look around—every day you owe, we owe the debt to this man Peter for many, many modern things—maybe we always need these tough guys—we are an empire, yes we are!—so how can we blame him alone! That would be the easy way out.

> *A beat.*

History is very complicated—also, it is very present—everywhere.

> *Putin, Patriarch, Pussy Riot...*

And also Peter he crushed the rebellion of his sister and put her to convent.

PUSSY RIOT MEMBERS. Men!

DEVOUT WOMAN. Better a convent than prison!

> *Pussy Riot is not so sure.*

SERGEI. *(To Guard.)* I, too, have a family.

GUARD. I know.

SERGEI. How do you—

GUARD. They come every day to see you and are turned away.

> *All hear this and are ashamed for their country.*
> *But the Pussy Riot case continues to rivet the West.*

DEFENSE. May I proceed?

JUDGE. Proceed.

DEFENSE. I have a list of witnesses to call.

JUDGE. Hmmf.

DEFENSE. I call on the patriarch.

> *The Patriarch hears this.*

JUDGE. Excuse me?

DEFENSE. The patriarch of the Russian Orthodox Church and friend to the president.

> *The Patriarch ducks out.*

JUDGE. He will not be called.

DEFENSE. Then I call on President Vladimir Putin.

JUDGE. Don't be ridiculous.

DEFENSE. I call on Vladimir Vladimirovich Pu—

JUDGE. You can't call on the president.

> *Blood seeps from under the Judge's stand.*
> *Everyone stares.*
> *Devout Woman tries to clean it.*
> *Judge covers it.*

You can't call on the president!

> *The strains of the Russian national anthem.*
> *Vladimir Putin himself, in a receiving line, shaking hands, waving.*
> *Flashbulbs go off.*
> *A red carpet unfurls before him.*
> *Putin's red tie matches carpet.*
> *Then anthem stops.*
> *HE is handling the case!*

PUTIN. When people push boundaries too far, it's not because they are strong but because they are weak.

Don't you think when people push boundaries too far it is because they are weak?

> *He does a quick "think fast!" judo move.*

But maybe weakness is not the worst quality for a woman.

> *Masked Pussy Riot are interviewed.*

NADYA. Pussy Riot.

KATYA. Pussy Riot.

MASHA. Pussy Riot.

REPORTER. This is the name of your group in English?

NADYA. It is only in English.

REPORTER. What do you mean?

NADYA. It is a very dangerous word in Russia.

KATYA. It is hard to explain.

REPORTER. How's that?

NADYA. Say it.

REPORTER. Pussy?

NADYA. No. Riot. Rriiiooot.

REPORTER. Riot?

NADYA. Yes.

REPORTER. Excuse me?

NADYA. Dangerous word, "riot." Since 1825.

REPORTER. I see.

S/he is writing as fast as s/he can.

NADYA. The Decembrist uprising. Against Czar Nikolai. It is complicated, this word. "Riioot."

There is a harrumph from the Russian Language Professor in audience. Who?

REPORTER. What happened to the Decembrists in 1825?

NADYA. Killed. Tortured. Siberia.

A member of the Troupe comes from audience as a Russian Professor of Languages—she wears eyeglasses on a chain, a comfortable sweater, and a grim expression.

RUSSIAN LANGUAGE PROFESSOR. Decembrists? I try to sit here, be polite, but—I am Russian—yes. It is clear their audience is the West, foreigners who don't know better. I am Professor Natal— well, I don't need to give my name—but I have credentials, I teach at a prominent American university. The Decembrists spoke five languages, they were musicians, intellectuals—and these girls—no, no, no—spouting off hoping greatness rubs off on them—

No one was expecting this.
They are taken aback.
Sergei takes her on gently.

SERGEI. Okay, maybe they are a little young, a little excited. And also they didn't say they were like Decembrists, only that the word "riot" became—

RUSSIAN LANGUAGE PROFESSOR. What? The word "riot" only became important to Russia with the Decembrists? *(To Sergei.)* You know better.— *(To audience.)* They are stupid girls and they are manipulating everything—

What bias!

(To audience.) You don't know the language, do you, you don't know how silly is this—spectacle—they are playing you.

Pussy Riot members decide to lay out the Pussy Riot Instruction Manual.

PUSSY RIOT MEMBERS. *(Distributed.)* If they say—"Take off your masks!"

Do not do it!

If they say—"What is your name!"

Make up a name! Invent an address!

Take out your balaclava—like Batman—always have it with you. So when you get a call to fight injustice—

Practice kicks like this.

And punch like this.

Is this a good color?

No one should know who we are.

Make up a name for yourself.

Never tell the truth to a cop. Or to any agent of the Putinist regime.

The main conception, one of the main ideas of the group, to be anonymous. That's why the masks.

Why the bright colors?

Because we are bright!

Put on your mask!

You will feel like a person who can do everything.

You will find more courage and conviction.

You will find the power to do something.

Is it like being a superhero?

Yeah yeah it is like being Spider-Man—

Catwoman!

We are not frightened at all.

If they say—

"Take off your masks!"

Don't be scared!

If they say—

"What is your name!"

Don't be stupid. Make it up!

Put some chocolate in your bag in case you spend the night in jail.

Pyotr is juggling his PR campaign—and his many phones.

PYOTR. Really? You think you can get to her? Can we reach out to her people? Make sure you say they're feminists—they're a radical feminist Russian punk band. Show them the photos we took, the one where Nadya looks like—yeah, that one. Say they're in big, big trouble.

There is some truth to everything. Let's all get a word in to the audience while we can.

DEVOUT WOMAN. I thought these girls should get a week with a broom, cleaning some parks, but then I hear they are comparing their trial to Jesus—JESUS? Now they compare themselves to Christ / it is too much.

MASHA. When you are sitting alone in your cell, you feel you are with these dissidents, who also suffered—

NADYA. My cellmate even had a talk with Jesus she said. Well, why not? Putin compares himself to the czars and the patriarch agrees—

DEVOUT WOMAN. The czars are not the Christ. They are just very close friends, the czar. Christ. Like brothers.

MASHA. Christianity is full of light.

NADYA. We will not commit the sin of gloom.

KATYA. In the face of oppression, injustice, and profound bureaucratic absurdity,

NADYA. fun can be a revolutionary act.

Russian Language Professor is back, truly unimpressed.

RUSSIAN LANGUAGE PROFESSSOR. *(To audience.)* There is an

unbridgeable chasm between cultures. Remember that at least, if you are going to listen to this crap. I guarantee if they all spoke English, you wouldn't be so enamored—they take out every "mm" and "ah" in the translation, context gone, nuance out the window—

Putin is clearing his throat, demanding the floor back.

If Putin spoke English, you would see a different man—maybe he is too clever—or too stupid—or too clever—to learn it.

TV show intro music.
There is the background murmur of translation in earbuds.

REPORTER. Mr. President, with hindsight, do you think the case could have been handled differently?

PUTIN. Could you please translate the name of the band into Russian?

REPORTER. Mr. President?

PUTIN. Translate the name.

REPORTER. Pussy Riot? The punk band. I don't know what you call them in Russia. Maybe you could tell me.

PUTIN. Please translate the first word into Russian. Or maybe it would sound too obscene? Yes. I think you wouldn't do it because it sounds too obscene, even in English.

REPORTER. Actually I thought it was referring to a cat but maybe I'm missing the point.

PUTIN. I know you understand it perfectly well. You don't have to pretend you don't get it.

REPORTER. We've brought an expert in from University of Bristol's Gender Research Centre to explain.

A British Feminist Lecturer speaks.

BRITISH FEMINIST LECTURER. Let's take this apart. First, "PUSSY"—Crude slang for the female genitalia—the area is, in fact, soft, warm, enveloping—and then the surprise, the jarring "RIOT"— disorder, chaos, disobedience.

The compliance of females, whether it be forced, coerced, or willing— is at the nexus of human history, because the womb is the factory of reproduction, and the means to the end for the survival of the species.

Gunshots.
Is the Lecturer shot?

The Reporter—and everyone else—takes cover.
Everyone except Putin.

LIEUTENANT. Examples must be set. Traitors punished. It is not an easy job, ruling an empire.

PATRIARCH. Vladimir Putin—and this Putin Era—is a miracle from God himself.

Marilyn Monroe, or the Troupe, sings "Happy Birthday, Mr. President."

Anna Politkovskaya, a journalist in glasses with short graying hair and a laptop, takes the space. Anna P. types, finishing her last article in her kitchen.

ANNA P. What reasons do I have to dislike Putin? There are many.

Can it be her?

TROUPE. What is your name?

ANNA P. Anna.

TROUPE. *(Distributed.)* Karenina?

Akhmatova?

ANNA P. Politkovskaya.

There is a gasp.

TROUPE. Date of birth?

ANNA P. 30 August 1958.

TROUPE. What is your name?

ANNA P. Anna Politkovskaya.

It is her.

TROUPE. Occupation.

ANNA P. Journalist.

Sergei speaks to audience—and Anna.

SERGEI. We have not been good to our Annas.

ANNA P. May I continue? Yes. There are many reasons.
His cynicism and racism. His endless wars and lies. The billionaires have his ear, and the people do not. This country is owned by corrupt businessmen—

REPORTER. What do you think of Pussy Riot?

ANNA P. Who is Pussy Riot?

REPORTER. In February 2012, on the eve of Putin's reelection—

ANNA P. In 2012, Putin is still president?

PUSSY RIOT MEMBER. It is now [insert current year, as long as Putin is still president].

KATYA. And he is STILL president.

ANNA P. No way!

TROUPE. Way.

ANNA P. *(Matter-of-fact.)* I didn't know. I was assassinated on the 7th of October in 2006, in the elevator of my apartment block. A Makarov pistol and four shell casings were beside my body. Reports indicated a contract killing, as I was shot four times. Once in the head.

> *A beat.*

It was Putin's birthday.

> *The birthday song begins again.*

The coincidence did not go unnoted.

> *Four shots are fired.*
> *The song stops abruptly.*
> *Anna P. is shot.*
> *She is speaking as if at a lecture, not her funeral.*

I do not like him because he does not like us.

> *She catches Putin's eye.*

These are appalling stories. What matters is the information, not what you think about it.

> *Devout Woman is gathering berries.*

DEVOUT WOMAN. Even so, it is a beautiful country. We have berries in the forests, so many varieties we have stopped naming them!

GUARD. We are the largest country in all the world, eleven time zones, stockpiles of weapons, the largest in all the world!

ANNA P. The question is not "Who did it?" but "Why was it done?" What intellectual and spiritual aberrations are at the heart of such a horrible crime? Dostoevsky, *Crime and Punishment*.

PUTIN. I love Russia.

MASHA. I love Russia.

LIEUTENANT. Everyone knows the world's best literature is Russian literature.

ANNA P. I love Russia.

KATYA. I love my country.

GUARD. I am a patriot.

> *Sergei is given and refuses another plate of food.*

SERGEI. Well, this is what we have.

> *The trial continues and the Devout Woman testifies.*
> *Judge peers out at audience.*

JUDGE. All these witnesses are for the prosecution?

PROSECUTOR. *(Motions to section of audience.)* These are the victims who filed charges against you.
So many. *(To Nadya, Masha, and Katya.)* Look at how many people you've insulted, huh?

> *The Devout Woman is among the victims in the audience.*

DEVOUT WOMAN. I was there.

JUDGE. The witness will speak!

DEVOUT WOMAN. I work at the cathedral.

JUDGE. So you are a victim! You have suffered!

DEVOUT WOMAN. Such disrespect! Such filth!

> *Judge and Prosecutor are competing to see who can be most*
> *appalled by these terrible crimes!*
> *Anyone can voice an opinion!*
> *Masha has been straining to hear.*

MASHA. I am Orthodox! I thought the church loved all its children but now I see it only loves those who love Putin!

DEVOUT WOMAN. Oh, God DOES love all of you, / every one!

PROSECUTOR. Did you explain to them that females cannot go up on the altar?

> *Unheard by court, Pussy Riot members voice their opinion*
> *again.*

PUSSY RIOT MEMBERS. Why not?

DEVOUT WOMAN. I begged them.

DEFENSE. Is it your job to—

DEVOUT WOMAN. It is not a job!

DEFENSE. You mean you receive no salary?

JUDGE. It is NOT your turn to ask questions.

DEFENSE. *(To Devout Woman.)* Have you yourself ever been on the altar?

DEVOUT WOMAN. Well…

DEFENSE. Maybe to clean it?

DEVOUT WOMAN. Somebody has to clean it!

DEFENSE. I see. So women are allowed on the altar.
Yes they are allowed as long as they are cleaning it!

> *Some laughter.*

DEVOUT WOMAN. *(Hurt, almost to herself.)* Are they laughing at me?

JUDGE. Remove anyone who laughed. No laughing in this court!

> *The Judge is satisfied.*
> *Devout Woman is relieved that is over.*
> *She didn't ask for this spotlight.*
> *She was subpoenaed.*
> *The Patriarch weighs in.*

PATRIARCH. No one has suffered as these women have. They have made soup when there was no meat, made warmth without heat, made life in the midst of war. Every Russian knows this. They have EARNED the respect of the people.

JUDGE. Thank you. *(To audience.)* All right. All of you! Please answer the prosecutor's questions. Can you do that?
Nice and loud so everyone can hear!

PROSECUTOR. Did you hear these girls kick, punch, and scream:

NADYA, MASHA, and KATYA. "Holy Shit!"

PROSECUTOR. Again and again? And was this offensive?
Was it appropriate for church?

AUDIENCE VICTIMS. […]

JUDGE. Do you think Nadya, Masha, and Katya have repented?

AUDIENCE VICTIMS. […]

> *If Audience Victims refuse to speak, Prosecutor and Judge must ad-lib on their behalf!*

PROSECUTOR. One of our witnesses has a statement she'd/he'd like to read into the record.

> *Prosecutor gives an Audience Victim a paper to read from. The Audience Victim reads from paper, or doesn't, depending on how willful or compliant the audience member is.*
> *If they refuse, the Prosecutor may read it in a disguised voice. Whatever it takes!*

AUDIENCE VICTIM. *(Reading aloud.)* "We will all forgive you—if you admit your guilt."

JUDGE. Thank you. Thank you all.
No more questions.

DEFENSE. But I haven't cross-examined them—

JUDGE. Well, you missed your chance.

MASHA. *(Towards Judge.)* Didn't you receive my motion last month? Requesting visits from my child? My mother?

> *Devout Woman doesn't know how to justify this but tries.*

DEVOUT WOMAN. How can you trust a woman who doesn't take care of her children?

NADYA and MASHA. *(To Devout Woman.)* We are in jail!

PROSECUTOR. There are no politics; they are just hooligans—

DEFENSE. I want to call—

JUDGE. No more witnesses.

DEFENSE. But—

JUDGE. This part of the trial is finished.

DEFENSE. These girls are not hooligans.

> *Sergei is watching everything so closely now.*

SERGEI and DEFENSE. And Nadya requires a doctor.

> *Judge has only heard Defense.*

JUDGE. On what basis?

DEFENSE. They have not eaten or slept, she is having trouble breathing.

JUDGE. Nonsense.

DEFENSE. You can see—

JUDGE. I have a piece of paper right here that says she is medically fit.

DEVOUT WOMAN. She looks a little pale!

DEFENSE. What is the date on this paper?

JUDGE. It is signed by a doctor.

DEFENSE. Are you denying her right to medical—

> *Back in prison, Sergei has been on hunger strike for some time.*
> *It begins to alter his reality, and the reality of the play shifts too.*

SERGEI. Doesn't it say that somewhere in my papers—

DOCTOR. I need to hear your answer. For the form.

SERGEI. Fourteen. Yes, fourteen days.

DOCTOR. You have lost four kilos.

SERGEI. What to do?

DOCTOR. It is a crime against life, what you are doing.

SERGEI. It is a crime to say—"No pictures! No protests! No thinking!"—

DOCTOR. I have a job to do—

SERGEI. —to Obey!

DOCTOR. to keep you alive—Let me do it.

> *A beat.*

You don't want to die, do you?

SERGEI. No I do not.

DOCTOR. You want to see your children grow up, take care of your mother, love your wife—

> *The Devout Woman is listening and Sergei knows it.*
> *Is it his mother? A stranger?*

DEVOUT WOMAN. How easily a man forgets his responsibilities!

SERGEI. But I never forget! I am locked up here!

DEVOUT WOMAN. That's why protesters are young! They have nothing to lose.

DOCTOR. It is a pity. I know.

> *Doctor sniffs Sergei's breath.*
> *The breath of someone who is starving becomes sickly sweet.*

It has been explained to you what will happen?

> *Sergei shrugs.*

If you continue?

SERGEI. More or less.

DOCTOR. Okay.

> *Attention shifts back to the court and the famous trial.*

JUDGE. Would the defendants like to say something?

DEFENSE. They have prepared closing statements.

JUDGE. I suppose they want to read them.

DEFENSE. They—do, yes. They want to read them into the court record.

> *Sergei interjects.*

SERGEI. They have something to say! They are burning to say it!

> *The Judge never hears Sergei.*

JUDGE. Are they long?

DEFENSE. Yes.

JUDGE. Well, what can be done about that.

> *Maybe a whispered conversation between Prosecutor and Judge.*

They will abbreviate them.

NADYA, MASHA, and KATYA. What?

JUDGE. You will abbreviate them!

> *Dissent from Pussy Riot.*

Okay, a short break and we will hear the abbreviated closing statements.

> *The entire country gets involved, egged on by their president.*

REPORTER. A public opinion poll released today says that fifty-six percent of the people say:

CROWD. Punish them!

PUTIN. Make no mistake, if the band, let's say, defiled a sacred place in Israel, they would have to cope with some tough guys there—

CROWD. Punish them!
Punish them!

REPORTER. Twenty-three percent say:

CROWD. *(Half the voices.)* They are innocent!

PUTIN. But if they defiled a Muslim shrine, security wouldn't have enough time to protect them from public anger.

JUDGE. *(From crowd.)* Little cunts!

> *This startles everyone.*
> *Even Putin is startled.*

PUTIN. I hope the court does not judge them too harshly… anyway, the decision rests with the court.

> *We are on TV.*

RUSSIAN TV HOST. A sin must be called a sin not a performance not a political action—

> *Claps and cheers.*

They're demons.
Am I supposed to forgive them?
Or first, punish them?

> *He punishes them.*
> *He may even bring the Cossack's whip out.*
> *He may even BE the Cossack.*

And then maybe forgive them, if they ask for it?

> *Back to public opinion.*

REPORTER. Twelve percent say:

CROWD. *(Two voices.)* Don't ask me!

REPORTER. And nine percent say they are "happy to abdicate all responsibility for everything."

> *TV continues to blare.*

RUSSIAN TV HOST. They are in jail! Good!
Send them to Siberia! Bravo!

CROWD. Punish them!
Punish them!

At last, back to court.

JUDGE. Quiet! Quiet. The defendants will make their closing statements.

NADYA. The cost of taking part in history is always staggeringly high for people. But that taking part is the very spice of life.

Judge "abbreviates" Nadya's speech.

JUDGE. Thank you. Enough! Samutsevich?

They are startled, but make the best of it. Katya stands.

KATYA. The whole world now sees that—

Judge bangs cudgel.

JUDGE. Thank you—
Enough!

The crowd reacts.
Masha stands without being called.

MASHA. Nobody can take away my inner freedom.
This freedom goes on living with every person who is not indifferent, who hears us in this country.

JUDGE. Thank you—

MASHA. *(Rolls over her.)* With everyone who found shards of the trial in themselves. I believe that I have honesty and openness, I thirst for the truth—

JUDGE. Thank you—

Masha will not be stopped.

MASHA. and these things will make all of us just a little bit more free. We will see this yet.

The crowd reacts.
Nadya and Katya clap.
Perhaps the whole room cheers and claps.

JUDGE. Keep your emotions to yourself. You were all told this. It is time to go. We will go home. And tomorrow we come back and I will read—I mean I will obtain—I will, um, render, the verdict.

TROUPE. What?

58

DEVOUT WOMAN. Who am I to judge? Christ says this many, many times.

TROUPE. How many?

DEVOUT WOMAN. Ach. No one will sleep tonight!

A pile of snoring yurodivy, Judge on top.

In prison:
Doctor is examining Sergei.
Guard nearby.
At first they do not speak.

DOCTOR. Twenty-two days. How do you feel?

SERGEI. Sad.

Doctor continues examination.

DOCTOR. How is your vision.

SERGEI. X-ray.

DOCTOR. Please respond without joke.

SERGEI. Okay. Clear.

GUARD. *(Interrupts.)* His vision is fine.

DOCTOR. I have a job to do.

SERGEI. It's fine.

DOCTOR. You say you are sad.

Doctor becomes personal.

Are you a believer?

SERGEI. Does it matter?

DOCTOR. I would send a priest.

SERGEI. For last rites?

Guard hears this.

DOCTOR. To talk.

SERGEI. I would prefer—a fair trial.

DOCTOR. That is not my domain.

SERGEI. Books, then. I would like books.

DOCTOR. Do you have delusions? Paranoia?

Sergei smiles.

SERGEI. Forgive me, I was born in Cold War era. Paranoia is normal.

A beat.

GUARD. Two minutes.

SERGEI. I do think we—what is the life for? I have time to ask these questions.

Guard is listening.

DOCTOR. Be careful.

SERGEI. My wife. She always says this.

A beat.

How to be sensible? How to be careful.
I don't think this is life.
I think we are lucky because we have this question—what is life?
When we ask it, we find courage.

DOCTOR. I will have them bring you something to eat.

SERGEI. I will eat when I am free to go to market and have chocolate and rugala.

Pyotr cuts through this moment.
He is outside court in heated phone conversation. He is in perpetual pursuit of attention that might save Pussy Riot.

PYOTR. The cover? Fantastic—keep pushing… I have back-to-back—Hold on I have to take this…

Another call.

She's coming in from the airport now? I'll meet you guys. Right…

Back to first call.

Guess where I'm headed right now—her hotel. This is going to be huge… Yes, court is in session, but what can I do there but sit on my ass and listen to testimony… The verdict is already written.

The Troupe weigh in.

SERGEI. The verdict is written.

PUSSY RIOT MEMBERS. The verdict is already written?

PUTIN. *(Clears throat.)* It's for the courts to decide.

JUDGE. The court will decide when it is written!

TROUPE. *(Distributed.)* Ha!

She is receiving direct instructions from Putin!

JUDGE. What?! It's a paranoia, where you see Putin behind every bush. It's like a medical condition.

Pyotr is still on that important call.

PYOTR. The press attention will keep them from getting killed. Yes, you can quote me. And, man, tell her we're all big fans. Sure.

Court is back in session.

JUDGE. Please state your full name.

NADYA. Tolokonnikova, Nadezhda Andreevna

KATYA. Samutsevich, Yekaterina

JUDGE. Date of birth.

NADYA. 7th November 1989

KATYA. 9th August 1982

JUDGE. Maria Alyokhina—

Masha stands.

What is your name?

MASHA. You just said my name. You know my name.

JUDGE. Of course we know your name! We are sick and tired of your name! But you must read it into the record. Say it again!

MASHA. Alyokhina, Maria Vladimirovna.

JUDGE. Date of birth.

MASHA. 6th June 1988.

JUDGE. What is your place of birth.

MASHA. Moscow.

KATYA. Moscow.

NADYA. The town of Norilsk.

Devout Woman can't keep quiet for long.

DEVOUT WOMAN. This one probably wants prison, wants the attention!

JUDGE. Children?

MASHA. A boy. Five years old.

NADYA. A daughter. Gera. She is four.

KATYA. None.

JUDGE. Occupation.

MASHA. Student.

NADYA. Artist.

KATYA. None.

JUDGE. Samutsevich,
This court finds you—

KATYA. I did not jump, pray, or sing.

JUDGE, PROSECUTOR, MASHA, and NADYA. What?

KATYA. I didn't jump, pray, or sing—

JUDGE. Speak up.

KATYA. We are a group but—I was removed from the altar before I had the chance to begin.

JUDGE. Hmm.

KATYA. I didn't perform any of the acts with which we were charged. I was pulled away by the security forces.

PROSECUTOR. Why didn't you say so?

JUDGE. You wanted to begin.

KATYA. Yes.

JUDGE. But you were prevented from doing so?

KATYA. Yes.

PROSECUTOR. This is good that you spoke up.

Everyone has an opinion about that.

DEVOUT WOMAN. It's true—but she should stick with the others!

PUSSY RIOT MEMBERS. Prison's no joke!

GUARD. If she can get out, she should get out!

PUSSY RIOT MEMBERS. She didn't commit any crime.

Pussy Riot reacts.
Katya forges ahead.

KATYA. It was all on the video. You all watched the video...

PROSECUTOR. How come it took so long to notice that?

Prosecutor and Judge confer.

The Defense walks in, busy on his phone with Pyotr.

DEFENSE. *(To Pyotr, on phone.)* Tonight? You're kidding. Can you get me a ticket?

He finishes call.

What did I miss?

JUDGE. Samutsevich says she didn't do anything.

Masha hugs Katya.

DEFENSE. What?

JUDGE. Apparently, she didn't do anything wrong.

PROSECUTOR. She wanted to—

JUDGE. But she was stopped before she could do it.

DEFENSE. That's not what we—

JUDGE. Nadezhda Tolokonnikova—Guilty.
Maria Alyokhina you are guilty!
Guilty!

The Judge confers with someone. Maybe a text, a phone call. Then.

Samunva/Satsuma—

Judge has forgotten her name already.

KATYA. Samutsevich.

JUDGE. What are you waiting for? You are free to go.

KATYA. I have a statement I'd like to—

JUDGE. You're free. You don't get to make any more of those.

Katya is removed from court.

PROSECUTOR. Your protesting days are over.

Defense is kind of stunned.
This had nothing to do with him.

DEFENSE. I'm kind of stunned.

JUDGE. Tolokonnikova! Alyokhina! You are deprived of your freedom for two years. The sentence is to be served in a penal colony.

CROWD. Shame! Shame!

The court erupts.

JUDGE. Quiet! Stop misbehaving!
Show respect for the court!
Two Years!

> *Outside the courts.*

VOICES FROM CROWD. *(Distributed; passing message down the line of supporters.)* Two Years!

Two Years!

Oh No!

A Deuce!

CROWD. Shame! Shame! Shame! Shame!

> *Audience encouraged to join in.*

SECURITY 1. Stop violating the social order.
If you've got a balaclava, pass it here!

CROWD. Shame! Shame! Shame! Shame!

> *A Pussy Riot supporter's sign is unfurled: "Your Honor, what happened to your HONOR!"*
> *Katya is swarmed when she gets outside the court.*

REPORTER. Katya, tell us why you were released?

KATYA. You tell ME why we were imprisoned.

REPORTER. Do you think the authorities intended to break up Pussy Riot?

KATYA. Pussy Riot is an idea.
We are not a band. We can't break up.

> *Nadya and Masha are sent to jail.*
> *Prisoners are punished.*
> *Nadya and Masha are in prison.*
> *Everyone standing in the yard, no one able to use the bathroom. No one able to take a sip of water.*

LIEUTENANT. *(To the assembled, including the audience.)* You're forbidden to have tea and food, from taking bathroom breaks, and smoking. *(Threatening, close to Nadya.)* If you weren't famous you would have had the shit kicked out of you a long time ago. Stay in the yard till lights out.

NADYA. It is freezing.

All are cold.

LIEUTENANT. *(Sniffs the air, pulls on his gloves.)* Yes?

Lieutenant approaches Nadya…

If you want to be paroled, you should play nice.

NADYA. I will report this.

Lieutenant turns to fellow Prisoner.

LIEUTENANT. Give me your boots.

Nadya sees this, starts to take off her own boots.

Not you. *(Points to Prisoner.)* You!

NADYA. What the—?

LIEUTENANT. *(To Prisoner.)* Take off your boots.

Prisoner takes them off and hands them to Guard.

(To Nadya.) I don't think you will ever complain again.

Nadya is still standing, shivering in the cold. The other Prisoner stands in her stocking feet.

REPORTER. "Brave"! "Heroic"! These are some of the words used to describe Puss—

MASHA. I don't know if it's brave. You just have to look around where you see injustice, and be willing to put on a balaclava and be arrested.

NADYA. And go to jail, be separated from your kids, lose your place, some of—

She sees Katya.

KATYA. Most of—

NADYA and KATYA. your friends.

MASHA. …Or be whipped or have acid thrown at you.

REPORTER. Nadya, do you believe artists have a duty to be active politically?

NADYA. It's not duty. It's reality. If you aren't thinking about politics, politics will think about you.

Masha is on intake at another prison.

LIEUTENANT. Take a chair.

MASHA. Thank you.

Lieutenant pulls on surgical gloves.

LIEUTENANT. Now open your legs.

MASHA. What?

LIEUTENANT. You can stash anything in there. Open.

The sound of an open-air concert across the city night.
The thumping beat of—could it be—

REPORTER. The messages are pouring in from celebrities around the world denouncing today's verdict: "We believe in you!" "Stay Strong!"— *(Reads a tweet.)* oh, I don't think I can say THAT one on live television! Anyway, folks out there are angry, but they haven't lost their sense of fun, the sense of rock-n-roll.
This just in: Yoko Ono: "Putin, give peace a chance."

A tickertape of tweets from celebrities supporting Pussy Riot:
Sting, Paul McCartney, Boy George, Bono, Patti Smith, Tobi
Vail...

CROWD. Svoboda Pussy Riot!
Freedom, Freedom!
Oh my God! MADONNA!

REPORTER. Oh my God! MADONNA!

Madonna's concert is attended by thousands of Muscovites.
Pyotr and Defense are in audience.
Hell, everyone except Nadya, Masha, and Katya are enjoying
the show!
And Madonna is putting on quite a show.
Then for the moment Pyotr has been planning for weeks...

MADONNA. *(At first breathless from dancing.)* I'd like to thank Pussy Riot for making the word "pussy" a sayable word in my household. It was once in the illegal-word category with my two eight-year-olds and now they go around saying "pussy" all the time—thanks for messing with my shit, ladies.
I decided to speak out tonight on your behalf—
Nadya. Masha. Katya.

A cheer.

Shh. A moment. Respect.

A dramatic pause, then she carries on.

I couldn't keep quiet when I heard—all of you—my fans here in Russia—can be arrested just for "gay behavior"—now that's just not right. Boo! I say Boo!

TROUPE. Boo!

MADONNA. And in case you don't think I'm serious I want you to know I've doubled my security in case what I'm about to do causes any—trouble.

TROUPE. We love you, Madonna!

MADONNA. I always saw myself as a freedom fighter and I have definitely paid for and been punished for speaking my mind. I truly believe we have a moral obligation to stand up for anyone being persecuted down the street or on the other side of the world.

She takes off jacket, reveals bejeweled black bra.

And I feel lucky to live in a country where I can do what I feel, wear what I want, and say what I think—for now, anyways!

She turns around.
FREE PUSSY RIOT is written across her back.
The stadium erupts.
Mostly yeahs but also some boos.
All types love Madonna.
She looks over shoulder to crowd.

Can I get a hell yeah

Yeahs.

A hell yeah

Yeahs!

A hell motherfuckin yeah

Wild yeahs!
Pyotr and Defense fist-pump.
Yes. She did it. She really did it.
Pyotr got her to do it. This is huge.
The music pulses, then fades.
The fog machine from the concert turns to the steam from the Russian baths. Putin and the Patriarch have a shvitz.

PUTIN. Aaahhh.

PATRIARCH. Aahhh.

A moment to soak in the heat.

Woman must be focused inwards, where her children are, where her home is. If this is destroyed then everything will be destroyed—

PUTIN. Of course, it's better not to argue with women…

PATRIARCH. I consider the phenomenon called feminism very dangerous. That could lead to the destruction of Russia.

PUTIN. Personally I believe that our Russian woman are the most talented and the most beautiful women in the world. I like all Russian women.

PATRIARCH. It's not for nothing that we call Russia the motherland.

Putin and the Patriarch contemplate the future of the motherland.

The British Feminist Lecturer (or is it her ghost?) emerges from the steam.

BRITISH FEMINIST LECTURER. "PUSSY RIOT": dangerous, unsettling, in ways even its young members do not realize. If ever there was a real, global "Pussy Riot," riot of the pussies, the world would be unrecognizable within a generation.

Toweling off after the baths, Putin arrives at interview shirtless…

He keeps practicing judo kicks with a sparring partner, unsettling the poor Reporter, who has had quite a time of it already.

REPORTER. President Putin, *Forbes* named you as the most powerful person in the world. Are you flattered by this?

PUTIN. You know, I am an adult. And I know what power means in the modern world. And Russia is the largest country in the world. It would be quite difficult to surround it.

REPORTER. It has been said that you have one foot in the old way of doing business and one foot in the / new.

PUTIN. *(Dismissive.)* We do not spread our legs.—

REPORTER. People are saying that freedom of speech is on its last / le—

PUTIN. We do not spread our legs.

Putin takes his leave.

Excuse me.

Putin returns.

I will add that I believe I am the wealthiest man, not just in Europe but in the whole world because I have the love and trust of the people. That is my true wealth.

He clears his throat, starts to hum and plink out a few bars of an American ballad like "Blueberry Hill."*
Putin performs the song in English.
And the Troupe sing along at the chorus.
Audience encouraged to use flash photography and clap, sing, and dance.
Everyone loves Putin!
Putin ad-libs, working the crowd.
Here the Troupe become Prisoners.
And Prison Guards.
The Prisoners all work in the labor camp.

MASHA. Now I realize that prison is just society—in miniature. It is designed to strip man of his individuality

PRISONERS. *(Distributed.)* —you get used to it quickly—

People begin to place high value on little nothings. A tablecloth—plastic dishes.

Outside, you have social status, which people value a great deal. I have never understood this.

Slowly, if you are paying close attention, you become aware of this government, of everything in your whole damn life, functioning as a performance, a play.

All of the yurodivy recognize this moment.

Nadya and Masha exchange letters.
They are passed around and read by Troupe.

MASHA. I don't know if this will reach you, Nadya—

NADYA. They will all read this letter even if it gets to your hands, dear Masha—

---

* See Note on Songs/Recordings at the back of this volume.

MASHA. I am writing to tell you I've again been transferred to yet another prison outside Moscow, where I can cause less trouble.

NADYA. If I file a complaint, all the women are punished.

> *Prisoners are punished.*

MASHA. I have been put in solitary to protect me from the others—

NADYA. I am sewing police uniforms—ha.

MASHA. I am sewing mittens.

NADYA. Nothing is adequate to the cold.

KATYA. My letters are returned to me unopened.

MASHA. I miss my son.

NADYA. I miss my daughter. I miss—

> *The worlds of the play continue to collide. Sergei is deep into his hunger strike and his illusions become part of the play.*

SERGEI. My children.

DOCTOR. You must live.

SERGEI. I must have something to live for.

> *The Doctor visits Sergei.*
> *Goes through the routine.*

My specialty, my friends, is the past. Now, at the close of the twelfth century, Genghis Khan and the Mongol hordes—

DOCTOR. What year is it?

SERGEI. It is of so very little, little consequence…

DOCTOR. How many days now?

SERGEI. Many, many…

TROUPE. *(Quietly.)* How many?

SERGEI. Genghis Khan, he did make many wars, kill many millions, but also they say half of Asia is descended from this man, that means—

TROUPE and SERGEI. What a guy!

SERGEI. It is very old history—a happy story, full of hope—you will celebrate with me.

> *Pussy Riot prepare for childbirth. Maybe they are very, very pregnant, holding their backs, trying to get comfortable, use breathing techniques. Supporting one another.*

70

It is about Woman, about how we enter this—a tribal woman, on the steppes, had an infant, a boy—it was little Genghis—

> *Genghis Khan is born.*
> *It is a difficult one!*
> *Devout Woman comes to help and enlists yurodivy assistance.*

There is only one way into this world.

> *The baby is held.*

And oh, many centuries pass, and on 3rd September 1530, comes Ivan the Terrible!

> *Ivan is born.*

He united all of Russia and in a rage killed his own son.

> *The infant is bounced.*

Another hundred years and from the Romanov family, 1672, the arrival of Peter, Peter the Great.

> *Peter is born.*
> *The Devout Woman plays midwife.*

He was a very tall guy, too. Peter.
Okay he killed those with beards. Nevertheless.

> *Pussy Riot give birth again and again, tossing the czars forward*
> *through the tunnel of history…*

Three hundred more years pass, many wars pass, diseases, progress, trade and treaties, maps and missions, many children born, many buried—

TROUPE. *(Quietly, almost an aside, a mumble, an echo.)* How many?

SERGEI. —until in a cramped communal apartment in Leningrad on 7th October in the year 1952, our current czar entered this world. His maternal grandmother baptized him in secret—

> *Devout Woman plays this grandmother.*

TROUPE, SERGEI, and DEVOUT WOMAN. Shhh!

SERGEI. They were all afraid of Stalin, but more afraid of the wrath of God.

> *Putin is born.*
> *Sergei is losing it.*

DOCTOR. I am taking your pulse.

SERGEI. Ah.

DOCTOR. You still have a strong pulse.

> *"Happy Birthday" song again.*
> *Nadya, Masha, and Katya are holding the infants.*
> *Devout Woman is cleaning up after the births.*
> *Putin enters, humming the same song he sang in English.*

PUTIN. *(Humming.)*

Hmm hm hm hm (Genghis good morning!)
Hhhmmm hmmm hmm (Ivan, be strong!)
hmmmm hmmm (Peter!!)
Hmm hmm hmm hmm hmm

> *Putin plays with infant's toes and mangles the nursery rhyme.*

This little pussy went to prison
This little pussy was paroled
This little mmmm had roast beef
This little mmm had none
And this little pussy cried wee wee wee—

> *Putin and Sergei see one another as if for the first time.*

DOCTOR. I am taking your pulse.

SERGEI. Ah.

PUTIN. You still have a strong pulse.

> *The streets of Moscow.*
>
> *A glorious fanfare!*
>
> *Troupe members parade through with the Olympic circle symbols.*

REPORTER. A surprise announcement from the Kremlin: amnesty for Masha and Nadya of Pussy Riot—and thousands of other prisoners—just in time for the Olympic Games!

> *Nadya and Masha are freed. Sergei is not.*
> *The tickertape of "congratulations" tweets go by.*

MASHA. We had only two months left in prison.

NADYA. Who is behind this?

---

* See Note on Songs/Recordings at the back of this volume.

REPORTER. The West is riveted as these brave girls emerge from the gulag—looking—

The Reporter checks them out.

pretty good!

> *Everyone wants in on this party.*
> *There are cheers and boos.*
> *A press conference.*
> *Nadya and Masha together.*

Nadya! Masha! Smile!

They do not.

Do you find it ironic that you are now celebrated the world over for your youth and beauty—when your group began as

PUSSY RIOT MEMBER. anti-capitalist

feminist

anonymous

and punk.

NADYA. We did not take off our masks.

MASHA. The cops took care of that.

NADYA. Believe it or not, anyone can be Pussy Riot. Pussy Riot belongs to the world.

CROWD. We love you, Nadya!

> *Many flashbulbs.*
> *A frenzy of reporters.*
> *Nadya is drowned out.*

> *Pyotr leads the charge from his phone.*
> *There is the sense that his words are being fed to him by Nadya*
> *as Putin fed words to the Judge…*

PYOTR. "Amnesty." Yeah, ready?—here's the quote:

Nadya is murmuring the words, in his ear? Through a device?

"Our amnesty was as illegal as our conviction. It is a PR stunt. They're not fooling anyone." …What? Takes one to know one. Okay, I'll take that—you got me—

> *The low strains of the earlier fanfare underscore his words,*
> *which build to a crescendo/manifesto!*

but the truth is if it's not on the internet, it didn't happen. That's the way of the world. I didn't invent that.

Sergei is losing strength while they are interviewed.
The crowds push closer.
The reporters in their faces.
The audience take photos.
Now they are famous and they are free.

Back in prison, the Guard is reading a book Sergei gave him.
It is an intimate scene.

SERGEI. They forget me. Okay okay I know they don't forget but maybe nevertheless they don't remember.

GUARD. I heard them talking in the—they are worried you will die.

SERGEI. They are taking bets? Making a pool?

Guard is offended.

Forgive me. I am not right—

He points to his head.
A moment.

GUARD. I brought you chocolate.

Guard presses chocolate into Sergei's hand.

You said you would eat if you had some—

Sergei holds chocolate in his hand.

SERGEI. Thank you.

A pause.

GUARD. Eat.

Press conference.

REPORTER. What will you do next?

MASHA. We are not free till we are all free.

NADYA. We don't have your microphones. All we have is the street.

Masha and Nadya begin to put on balaclavas.

PUSSY RIOT MEMBERS. *(Led by Nadya.)* Vladimir!
Vladimir Vladimirovich Putin?

PUTIN. Yes.

Sergei attempts to stand.

He is not stable.
He is not in his right mind, but he is holding on.

PUSSY RIOT MEMBERS. Date of birth?

PUTIN. 7 October 1952.

SERGEI. 10 September 1961.

TROUPE. Speak up! What is your name?

> *Sergei tries.*
> *Pussy Riot help him.*

SERGEI. I am Sergei Barbarov of the protests of—

PUTIN. Everyone knows my name.

PUSSY RIOT MEMBERS. Place of birth?

> *Putin beats Sergei to these replies.*

PUTIN. Leningrad.

PUSSY RIOT MEMBERS. Employed?

> *A beat.*

PUTIN. Yes.

PUSSY RIOT MEMBERS. What is your profession?

> *Sergei beats Putin to the answer this time.*

SERGEI. History.

PUSSY RIOT MEMBERS. How do you plead?

PUTIN. I don't understand the charges.

PUSSY RIOT MEMBERS. How do you plead?

PUTIN. No one has read out the charges.

> *Pussy Riot looks around.*
> *There is a lot to charge him with.*
> *Where to begin?*

It seems that you are all denying my right to a defense.

> *Gunshots are fired.*
> *All duck except Putin—and Sergei.*
> *Putin looks at Pussy Riot.*

Everybody has an agenda. What to do?

ANNA P. "Find the person whose agenda it is to tell the truth."

SERGEI. —What is the main problem facing society. Our beloved Chekhov—he asked this question again and again—In his beautiful play *Uncle Vanya*, he asks—

Sergei sees Devout Woman is tending to him.

"One hundred years from now. One hundred years to the future: Will people look kindly upon us? Will they be proud of what we've done—"

He wants so badly to finish this thought.
He has nothing left.
He cannot finish.

DEVOUT WOMAN. "God always forgives—but people might not."

Devout Woman feels for his pulse. None.
She crosses herself.
The "Bogoroditse Devo" is sung, or plays, very softly at first.

GUARD. No photos. Please. And keep your emotions to yourself. It's just theatre.

He has to keep his own emotions to himself.
Sergei is gone.

KATYA. *(Masked.)* We are an idea.

MASHA. *(Masked.)* An idea feels no pain.

NADYA. *(Masked.)* An idea can live forever.

Sergei becomes yurodivy,
Devout Woman becomes yurodivy,
Putin, Madonna, Lieutenant, Judge…
Masha, Katya, Nadya.
All are yurodivy.

I'm [insert name here].

Each one follows suit and very simply says their real names and either their date of birth or their place of birth, echoing what Sergei, Putin, and Nadya, Masha, and Katya have done repeatedly…

TROUPE. *(One by one.)* I'm [insert name here].

I'm [insert name here].

I'm [insert name here].

> *This repeats till each cast member has said his/her/their name.*
> *They drop all semblance of "performing" but still claim Pussy*
> *Riot as theirs.*

(Distributed.) We are Pussy Riot.

We are P.R.

Everything is P.R.

We beg you not to forget.

> *The "Bogoroditse Devo" becomes louder and fills the space, as*
> *it did at the beginning of the play.*
> *At some point, the music changes to a Pussy Riot song.* *
> *The choral hymn breaks into punk.*

End of Play

---

* See Note on Songs/Recordings at the back of this volume.

PROPERTY LIST

(Use this space to create props lists for your production)

SOUND EFFECTS
(Use this space to create sound effects lists for your production)

Dear reader,

Thank you for supporting playwrights by purchasing this acting edition! You may not know that Dramatists Play Service was founded, in 1936, by the Dramatists Guild and a number of prominent play agents to protect the rights and interests of playwrights. To this day, we are still a small company committed to our partnership with the Guild, and by proxy all playwrights, established and aspiring, working in the English language.

Because of our status as a small, independent publisher, we respectfully reiterate that this text may not be distributed or copied in any way, or uploaded to any file-sharing sites, including ones you might think are private. Photocopying or electronically distributing books means both DPS and the playwright are not paid for the work, and that ultimately hurts playwrights everywhere, as our profits are shared with the Guild.

We also hope you want to perform this play! Plays are wonderful to read, but even better when seen. If you are interested in performing or producing the play, please be aware that performance rights must be obtained through Dramatists Play Service. This is true for *any* public performance, even if no one is getting paid or admission is not being charged. Again, playwrights often make their sole living from performance royalties, so performing plays without paying the royalty is ultimately a loss for a real writer.

This acting edition is the **only approved text for performance.** There may be other editions of the play available for sale from other publishers, but DPS has worked closely with the playwright to ensure this published text reflects their desired text of all future productions. If you have purchased a revised edition (sometimes referred to as other types of editions, like "Broadway Edition," or "[Year] Edition"), that is the only edition you may use for performance, unless explicitly stated in writing by Dramatists Play Service.

Finally, this script cannot be changed without written permission from Dramatists Play Service. If a production intends to change the script in any way—including casting against the writer's intentions for characters, removing or changing "bad" words, or making other cuts however small—without permission, they are breaking the law. And, perhaps more importantly, changing an artist's work. Please don't do that!

We are thrilled that this play has made it into your hands. We hope you love it as much as we do, and thank you for helping us keep the American theater alive and vital.

Note on Songs/Recordings, Images, or Other Production Design Elements

Be advised that Dramatists Play Service, Inc., neither holds the rights to nor grants permission to use any songs, recordings, images, or other design elements mentioned in the play. It is the responsibility of the producing theater/organization to obtain permission of the copyright owner(s) for any such use. Additional royalty fees may apply for the right to use copyrighted materials.

For any songs/recordings, images, or other design elements mentioned in the play, works in the public domain may be substituted. It is the producing theater/organization's responsibility to ensure the substituted work is indeed in the public domain. Dramatists Play Service, Inc., cannot advise as to whether or not a song/arrangement/recording, image, or other design element is in the public domain.

9780822239055